THE GHOST OWL SAYS GO NOW

STEPHEN BENZ

POETRY

STEEL TOE BOOKS
est. 2003

All Rights Reserved

Printed in the United States of America

First Edition
1 2 3 4 5 6 7 8 9

Selections of up to two pages may be reproduced without permission. To reproduce more than two pages of any one portion of this book write to Steel Toe Books publishers John Gosslee and Andrew Ibis.

Copyright ©2024 Stephen Benz

ISBN 978-1-949540-26-0

Steel Toe Books
steeltoebooks.com

For special discounted bulk purchases, please contact sales@steeltoebooks.com

THE GHOST OWL SAYS GO NOW

CONTENTS

ONE

Wanderlust	2
Haibun: Meridian, Mississippi	3
The Cat Hoarder	4
From Fitzgerald's Notebooks:	
"Driving over the rooftops on a bet"	6
En Route: Shreveport, Louisiana	8
American Naturalism	10
Pantoum: Off the Rails	12
En Route: Weatherford, Oklahoma	14
Tree of Life	15
Uncle Eddie's War Stories	18
Uncle Bill's War	21
Hopperesque	23
Double-A Pitching Change	31
Crossing New Mexico	34
Passing Through	37
I-10, Westbound	39

TWO

Haibun: Hitchhiking, First Ride	41
Starlight	42
Hitchhiking at Night	44
Pantoum: Down and Out	45
Many Detours	46
Road Kill	48
Elk Herd	50
Hitchhiker's Nightmare	51
Crossing Flagstaff	52
Poem Going Nowhere	53

THREE

Variations on Five Phrases from Susan Sontag	55
En Route: Apalachicola, Florida	57
Three Thousand Miles: A Haibun Sequence	58
Variations on a Theme from *North by Northwest*	64
Postmodern Western	65
Another Bad Day at Black Rock	67
En Route: Carrizozo, New Mexico	69
Uncle Jack's War Wound	71
Uncle Joe, AWOL in Bangkok	73
En Route: Beatty, Nevada	74
Ghost Towns Out West	76
The Donner Pass Diner	77
Birthplace	79
John Berryman, Encyclopedia Salesman	81
Land of Opportunity	83
Uncle Jerry, Missing in Action	85
Reaganomics: A Memoir	86
Fugue	88
So What	89
Southbound	90
Acknowledgements	96
About the Author	98

| | one | |

WANDERLUST

Once again you're taking the long way,
fooling with the radio dial
and idly reading the signs.

Almost There! Ten Miles Ahead!
Whether ten or a hundred, you don't care.
You're in it for the long haul, you tell yourself
moving on just for the sake of moving,
losing yourself in wanderlust.

Last Chance Gas. Pay no heed, push ahead.
It's the lost highway, no stopping now.
You'll get yours farther on.

Exit Now. In a blink you're past it
thinking nothing's wrong,
and the road ahead empties,

a shimmering mirage where
wanderlust knows no bounds.

HAIBUN: MERIDIAN, MISSISSIPPI

Meridian was where my passengers needed to go, three church ladies in pastel hats whose car had broken down alongside a tract of logged-out pine. They were fanning themselves in the shade when I stopped to offer help. *A Samaritan, praise be.* In Meridian there was a cousin with a tow truck. If I could deliver them to his garage, they'd be much obliged. Squeezed together in the backseat, they hummed a hymn and fanned, said that old car was nothing but trouble and the Lord works in mysterious ways.

In town, they directed me up and down humble streets and warned me not to stay too long in Meridian: "the devil's abode," the eldest assured me. I said I was hoping to get some lunch. In that case, they all agreed: I should go to Jean's place, down on Front Street by the train station. Ham and black-eyed peas, they suggested, then hymned their way on into the cousin's garage, Blessed Auto Repair.

Startled into flight
a flock abandons the roost.
Magnolia blooms fall.

THE CAT HOARDER

My mother is at wit's end with her neighbor.
When I come for a visit she says,
"Can't you do something, dear—all those cats.
And the smell, the filth, the poor woman's
gone plumb mad."

From an upstairs window I watch
the adjoining lot where cats—at least thirty—
loll in the sun of the unkempt yard.
One scratches at a pine tree trunk. Three more
pace nervously at the patio door, tails erect
and twitching. It's a motley collection: tabbies,
calicos, and tuxedos. A few torties mixed in.

When I cross the yard, the stink
getting stronger with each step,
five or six cats scamper off into bushes.
Two start up, then freeze in a tense crouch,
alert to the threat, ready to run. Up close,
I see mange, missing eyes, bit-off ears,
deep wounds oozing and infected.
There is mewling and hissing.
The dead grass is pocked with crusted piles.

No one answers my knock. I remember
when boyhood home runs crossed this fence,
and I'd jump over to fetch the whiffle ball.
The grass was thick and green back then,
and Mrs. Burke waved brightly from her window.
She had maybe two or three cats in those days.

But the feline silhouettes decorating her mailbox
and welcome mat suggested a fondness, and so
the neighborhood came to think of her as a cat lover.
When the Glenns moved away they left Rosie
with her. The Harwoods gave her kittens

from an unwanted litter. And at least twice
we kids brought her strays we had found,
surprised and impressed by her joy
and kindness upon taking them in.
"Oh, look at you, yes, just look at you,
little kitty, kitty, let's get you some milk,
there now you poor hungry thing."

I remember the pathos in her voice
as I look through the listings to find
the proper agency of city government
for handling the matter: Animal Control,
according to the blue pages. While the men
in white jumpsuits snatch the cats,
their long poles equipped with noose-like loops,
Mrs. Burke is bawling and beating her fists
against the porch rail, a wail that brings
neighbors to their doors. "Typical case,"
the lead agent of impoundment tells me.
"Old woman, all alone, no one to care,
just the cats. She fits the profile to a T.
Tragic, really, but far worse for the animals.
Most of these will have distemper or leukemia.
Bet we end up putting them all down." And then
he hands me the clipboard, pointing out the X
where I am supposed to sign,
confirming the Citizen's Complaint.

Next morning, well before dawn,
I am up making coffee. Through the screen
I see a beam outside in the darkness.
It's Mrs. Burke in bathrobe and slippers,
wandering the yard with a flashlight.
Just audible above the noise of night insects,
she's calling out in a hoarse voice: *Tabatha?*
Marlene? Henry? Jezebel? Sapphire?
Here, kitty, here kitty, kitty.

FROM FITZGERALD'S NOTEBOOKS: "DRIVING OVER THE ROOFTOPS ON A BET"

When it comes to a downfall
his can only make you wince,
nothing noble in it. In short order
he lost the job, lost the manuscript,
lost the car, lost everything
except decanter and pill case.
Zelda and Ernest occupied his thoughts
though he was long out of touch with both.

In the newsreel, he's outfitted with a chauffer's cap
and someone has foolishly given him the keys.
He guns the engine and goes clickety-clack
up and down gambrels and over
a set of Spanish tiles before crashing into a gable.
One cockeyed wheel spins and spins,
and it's just like that madcap scene from *Gatsby*
now reenacted in Hollywood Hills.
The rescue squad arrives to talk him down.
He claims he sees Hemingway
one ledge over cursing him for a blasted fool.

But what if he had somehow survived it all,
the pratfalls in pools, the headlong brawls
when he couldn't cover the check,
the agonizing bouts of writer's block.

What if he could have found his way out of the maze,
written the great novel of the fugue state
while holed up in the Skyland Hotel, scene
of his brutal crack-up, just a short drive from
Zelda's asylum, a short drive in a borrowed car
on back roads where, as he put it,
he had left behind all capacity for hope.

But no. The ending imminent, he lurked
in the bushes below her window, a fall-down Romeo
slurring his words, saying *Hey honey, hey ya doll,
I've got fifty dollars—make it a hundred—
says we can ride this jalopy across every shingle in town.
What do you say, sugar?* And what could Sugar
possibly say but what she'd said so often before:
*Oh Scott, you crazy, crazy, crazy son of a bitch—
Nothing, no one, could ever survive you.*

EN ROUTE: SHREVEPORT, LOUISIANA

Staring at the road through rain-streaked glass
brings on a headache that neither pills nor coffee has quelled.
And now a Waffle House break, that greasy smell
rising from the griddle where hash browns and bacon sizzle,
Country radio hardselling nostalgia and close-out furniture.
Just like the good old days. Everything must go.

Two waitresses on a cigarette break out back in the rain,
a third yawning as she pours coffee for the clientele.
Over in the corner booth, a debate in progress: prospects
for Tiger football after last Saturday's blowout in Tuscaloosa.
"You just can't keep throwing like that against a nickel D."
"You ask me they're a bunch of shiftless bums this year.
Ought to bench the whole lot, bring in new blood.
I mean, what are we looking at bowl-wise—Liberty?
Peach? The goddamn Peach Bowl. Shit."

The road map says there's a good three hundred miles to go.
Four, five hours yet, and this headache just won't quit.
Nor will the rain, a steady deluge all across the South.
In "The Narrow Road," Bashō writes,

*I felt three thousand miles
rushing through my heart,
the whole world only a dream.*

The two smokers have finished their break
and now stand behind the counter tying on aprons,
continuing a conversation from outside.

"All I'm saying, honey, is
you got to put your foot down some time,
tell him no."

"I know, I know, but easier said than done."

"Well, ain't that always the case? Stop with the excuses, or one of these times someone's going to get seriously hurt, and you know who."

AMERICAN NATURALISM

She was young, carefree. There were church picnics,
the wet taste of melon straight from the field,
one whole table chockfull of pies and cakes.
Playing tag, the children ran into the woods.
Something happened, and she was never the same.

In school, they practiced their sums. An ordeal
when called to the chalkboard, given problems
to solve under scrutiny. Winter wind
rattled classroom windows. The boiler hissed.
Something happened, and she was never the same.

"Lord, that child was stubborn, a regular mule.
Mother and daughter in a contest of wills.
It was going to end badly. These things do.
We were at wit's end and the Law was involved.
Something happened, and she was never the same."

The boys learned to drive; the bold ones stole cars.
There were malteds at the drive-in and joy rides
in the wasteland. An invitation to hop in.
Night sky. Stars. Dust settling at a dead end.
Something happened, and she was never the same.

A job with a law firm, the usual chores:
typing, filing, the daily grind, no breaks.
Friday nights, the Grifter Bar, she staked her place.
Sweet talk promised the moon, an easy way out.
Something happened, and she was never the same.

Morning sickness, queasy with a growing fear.
Office scandal, pay cut, finally the pink slip.
Where does a girl turn when the other shoe drops?
No choice: Someone knew a man who knew a man.
Something happened, and she was never the same.

The courthouse wedding was brief. No cake, no gown.
Just a fast drive up the coast, a dim motel.
She knew what was coming and didn't blink.
His hand over her mouth, on the nightstand a gun.
Something happened, and she was never the same.

Months on the move, one trailer court to the next.
Midnight phone calls, paraphernalia
on the kitchen counter, a fight always on boil.
A stranglehold pushed her over the edge.
At dawn, the sheriff's men, the mortuary hearse.

Something happened, and she was never the same.
Prejudicial evidence brought about the end:
a county courtroom, sobs, objections,
a brutal cross-exam. The judge duly polled
the jury: twelve dead-set men who sealed her fate.

PANTOUM: OFF THE RAILS

The family's just sick about it,
but what can be done now? He's gone.
Everyone knew he was an odd sort.
Still, what a shock for it to end this way.

But what can they do, now that he's gone?
All that's left is to wonder why? How?
Such a shock for it to end this way.
You knew he was off the rails, still—

All that's left is to wonder how and why.
The drugs, the fights, juvenile detention.
You knew he was off the rails. Still,
there's no helping someone who doesn't want help.

More drugs, more fights, detention, rehab.
He went through it all and then some.
You can't help someone who doesn't want help.
Then he goes and disappears all those years.

They say he did it all and then some,
spiraling downward, dealing with the devil.
He disappeared for years, somewhere
exotic like Bangkok, Goa, Cuzco.

A downward spiral, a deal with the devil:
clues pieced together from letters, postcards
stamped Thailand, India, Peru.
He was searching for something, no one knew what.

Peruse the letters and postcards for clues
and there's still enigma at the core.
He was searching for something. Who knows what.
They say he read scripture, all the holy texts.

Beneath the surface, he was pure enigma.
The family's just sick about it.
They say he studied scripture, all the holy texts.
Everyone knew he was an odd sort.

EN ROUTE: WEATHERFORD, OKLAHOMA

The town shut down early as the first flurries fell. Everyone had gone home long before I arrived, tooling down Main in heavy snowfall, looking for vacancy. I had trouble rousing the innkeeper, who seemed perturbed but still took my money and slid a cold key onto the counter only after scrutinizing the registration form, photocopying my ID, and holding the bills up to the light. Weatherford meant white-out and standstill, an overpriced, seedy room with faltering heat, an hour of flipping through insipid television channels before I dozed off. Come morning, snow had filled the streets. In the town center, drifts blocked doors and storefronts. On the outskirts, number 15 at the Wagon Wheel was banked with snow. When I opened the door, fine powder blew in and sparkled as it melted on the frayed carpet. Wonderful how a blast of winter clears the mind, how extreme cold crystallizes matters. In Weatherford that day, everything—the limbs of a barren tree, road signs, telephone wires, mileposts, a row of stranded boxcars—was glazed with ice to the point of startling clarity. But clarity was only in things: myself, I felt as leaden and obscure as ever. Once again, I had second thoughts about the decision to come this way, following the road of false nostalgia. Doubts piled with the snowdrifts. There were crossroads ahead, decisions to make, but for a long day and a half I was forced to wait until the plow came around to clear a path out of town. As always in the dubious hours, I thought of Bashō, his death poem:

> *On a journey ailing—*
> *my dreams wander*
> *over a desolate moor.*

TREE OF LIFE

At the time, I was too young to know anything
about the World Tree, but even then
I could well believe that our tree
was at the center of everything
and the source of something profound.

The tree watched over the greenspace
at the entrance to Fairwood,
the planned community where we lived.
Every day we gathered there,
six neighborhood boys passing
summer's slow hours perched on limbs
among the maple leaves. Our bicycles leaned
against the tree's trunk while up
in the branches we talked about
baseball, the Beatles, moon landings.

Sap rubbed onto our skin. Knots and gnarls
scraped us, sometimes drawing beads
of blood. But we didn't mind the scratches.
We didn't mind getting sticky.
The pleasures of tree-climbing
outweighed those brief irritations.

But this isn't a story about a tree per se.
It's the story of a man who appeared one day
at the base of the tree. A military man
in dress uniform calling up to us,
seeking our help in locating an address,
a house hard to find among Fairwood's many
identical cul-de-sacs. It happened
that I was lowest in the tree just then.
I swung from the branch and dropped
to the ground. He looked me in the eye
from beneath the brim and showed me

the address. I knew the street all right,
having ridden my bike around and around
the neighborhood a thousand times over
while delivering newspapers.

Getting to the house in question required
a somewhat convoluted course, a couple
of tricky turns to reach the right cul-de-sac.
Rather than trying to describe the way,
it seemed easier to guide him, riding ahead
on my bike while he followed in the car.
"All right, soldier," he said. "Lead the way."

Those were days of heavy heat, the dog days
of August. The asphalt seemed soft
beneath my tires, but I pedaled hard
to set the pace and lead the big black car
to its target. When we got there, I stopped
at the curb and pointed out the house.
The man gave me a casual salute.
I watched while he adjusted his hat
and marched to the door. It was a house
I knew from my paper route. The Hansons.
They were older, no kids my age. Their son
had been a high school basketball star
a few years back. The officer rang the bell
and waited, looking up at windows,
leafing through his notebook.
As he reached to ring the bell again,
the door opened. A woman appeared
at the threshold. Mrs. Hanson.

                        What next?
A potentially awkward moment,
but the officer was practiced at it.
Had done this before, and often.
Sitting on my bicycle, squinting
into sunlight, I watched, not knowing

then what it was all about—not exactly,
though I must have had an inkling,
given everything we saw on the news.
The officer removed his hat, said something.
Mrs. Hanson stood still, expressionless,
then moved aside to let him in,
and the door shut. I sat a moment
feeling the full heat of the day
then rode back to the tree,
pedaling slowly.

A while later, maybe twenty minutes,
our little group sat at the base of the tree.
Maybe we were drinking Cokes.
Maybe we were eating cookies
someone's mother had made. Maybe
we were pondering the rumors
of Paul McCartney's death or lamenting
the Cubs' late-summer swoon. The black car
came cruising toward us. As it approached,
the sun's glare on the windshield
prevented us from seeing the man inside—
only his arm out the window,
elbow resting on the frame,
fingers tapping the roof.
I remember his hand.

He passed us by and gave a friendly wave,
as if to say, "See you later, boys."

UNCLE EDDIE'S WAR STORIES

1. *Borderlands Outpost*
The day we attacked the village I took off
the headset and went up the tower to watch
with the nocks. Mortar exploded like seeds
from overripe pods. Ricky shouted,
Hombre! Look at that! Whoa!

Ricky: my friend from East L.A.
where the girls were so pretty, he said,
sitting on car hoods and combing
long black hair, singing siren songs.
Man, that's where I want to be, I said,
and Ricky laughed as if to say, No way,
puto, no way. You're never getting out
of here—not none of us.

Then one, two, three, four gunships
lifted up like insects and crossed the swamps.
Someone said they're going for the wounded,
and Ricky said nah, they're gonna strafe
the survivors running the road to the north.
Go get 'em, boys. *¡Andale, cabrones!*

At night, radio static was our white noise
muffling the mortar fire. We slept in our sweat,
Ricky tossing and groaning. He never slept well.

I tried to think of girls, those pretty girls
in East L.A., but when I closed my eyes
I saw only bomb-seeds spurting
like dandelions on an August day back home.

2. *What We Did*
About half a mile from the hamlet
we started a trench. The idea being,

Lieutenant Bullneck said, to find a place
close enough for us to haul the bodies
without too much effort, but far enough
so the frigging human rights hounds
and jag-off journalists wouldn't find shit.
A logistical nightmare, he called it.

He decided on this muddy embankment,
the far side of a canal. Bullneck ordered me
to pour out the lime. Did I complain?
No sir, not a word. The clouds of powder
stung my eyes, but I was glad
I was only hauling bags.
Myers, Sanders, and Duarte
he detailed to the village,
issued canisters and gas masks,
told them do it double time.

3. *Foraging in Enemy Territory*
After five days without a supply drop
the lieutenant sent us out to forage
in what remained of the villages.
Earth and air seethed with chemicals.

We coughed as we walked,
throats burning, bellies aching.
God damn it all, Ricky said
and let out a howl. Myers told him
to shut the hell up and did he
want every fucking sniper
to know we were coming?
The trees were all shredded and stripped,
the swamplands stagnant and fetid,
oily rainbows staining the water's surface.
What's the map say, they asked me,
and I made a show of reading it
though we all knew damn well
it was the same old worthless intel.

We found a village in the heat of day,
a collection of charred huts
circled around a well. Ricky pissed
into the well and Myers told him to stick
his goddamned cock back in his pants.
Ricky's laugh echoed in the empty village.

We found nothing—not a rooster, not a dog,
not so much as a kernel of rotted grain.
But in the last hut there was a girl,
naked, lying in thatch, her small breasts
and belly striped with dirt. She looked up
at us through animal eyes and babbled.
Myers said where is everybody?
Ricky talked Spanish to her.
The girl moaned. A lunatic, Myers said,
abandoned when her family fled the gunships.

Ricky parted her legs with his gun and stared.
Blood trickled from the girl. I had never
seen this before. Forget it, man, I said.

We reported our failure to the lieutenant,
who sure as hell wasn't pleased.
He climbed the tower and scanned the horizon,
said he gave us three days at best.

That night, I dreamed about the girl.
I saw her blood as food. I touched her
and licked my fingers. I knelt to bite her.
When I woke up in the dark
I was trembling and sick to my stomach.
Ricky held a flashlight above his Bible
and whispered verses from the Psalms.

UNCLE BILL'S WAR

He went along with shipmates to drink beer
in bars where disco lights flashed
to synthetic music while girls
shook and shimmied and gyrated
on tabletops, somehow keeping balance
despite spiked heels and valium cocktails.

Rain was constant, rain in Olongapo,
rain in La Hermita, rain so furious
it drew him from the disco lights
and the dancers and the barkeep's chatter
about Japanese baseball and the low,
low bar fine for the girls *You like? You like?*

He did not want girls. He only wanted to watch
the fearsome monsoon, marveling at the filth
its mad waters carried down the streets:
rotted fruit, chicken bones, dog shit,
bottles, cans, condoms, fish heads
swirling in the gutter rapids.

So he turned away from the girls
and stared out windows in the bars
that had windows, or stood at the doorway
squeezing a San Miguel by the throat,
rain splattering his Navy blues,
and for hours he watched
what the torrent carried past.
A doll's head. A straw sandal.
A carved water buffalo. A sailor's cap
blown off some drunk squid's head.

Once, during the height of the downpour,
runnels and riffles in the overflowing street,
the sodden corpse of a cat eddied past.
"Sweet Jesus," he said.

Behind him someone shouted,
What the hell are you looking at?
The girls giggled nervously,
the barkeep clucked *no good, no good,*
and his pals urged him back into the bar
where he could be spending his sailor's pay,
having a little fun and forgetting,
if only for the time being,
this fucked-up war and the many,
many ways it messed with your head.

HOPPERESQUE

The inner life of a human being is a vast and varied realm.
— Edward Hopper

1.
Now is the time for nuance,
probing for subtext. She recalls
he once used the word "standstill"
in a letter and she puzzled for days
at the cruel expression of his apathy.
That was before the ill-advised wedding,
before the feckless ocean crossing,
when boredom and close quarters
sapped all compassion. Now she reads
the latest missive for misgivings,
the subtle irony of regret, knowing
of course he will never come clean.

2.
One day there's hell to pay:
simple fact of anyone's life.
The foundation seems solid enough.
Four walls, a good roof,
the furnishings that make for comfort
and ease. But furnishings are also
trappings, and one day you wake up
trapped, whichever way you turn.
Tick, tick, tock. Long ago you colored
at the kitchen table while daddy
finished off the whiskey dregs.
"Son," he said. "You work, you drink,
you die. One day there's hell to pay.
That's all the wisdom your old pop's
got for you." You answered him
the way you were taught "Yes, sir."
And today, two years older than he was then,

you still don't have a better answer.
You stand in the backyard
as day goes dark thinking yes, sir,
one day there's hell to pay.

3.
His habit: watching the sea for
hours on end. No real purpose in it,
just what he feels compelled to do.
Water. Light. The smell of salt.
The warpage of the porch,
planks absorbing moisture.
It's all about time, the tide
sneaking up, falling back,
shadows in motion,
the day passing him by.

4.
The moment of recognition:
this is the place she cannot escape.
Not even walking out the door
would do the trick, a false threshold.
Light pours uninvited into the room,
cold and daunting, her nakedness exposed.
Shadows are implacable, the books
evoke phantoms. Bedstead. Writing desk.
Drought-stricken trees beyond the pane,
beyond her ken. Well into dotage,
her grandmother had a habit of saying,
"I'm in fine whack, praise God."
But no such lie will serve, not now, not here,
entrapped as she is, nothing to stave
off the worst of it, the light, these walls.

5.
Morning after a restless night.
The window admits harsh light,
and he is glad for the brutal glare,

the way each object declares itself
when lit up. Chair, book, bedclothes.
The world of bad dreams
temporarily banished,
a reassurance that *this*—not that
nightmare world—is reality.
All right, he tells himself, *all right.*
That's over for now and I'm still here,
still alive, for what it's worth.

6.
Dark windows
reveal nothing
of the life inside.
Light can bestow
dimension—
or steal it.
Sudden
luminosity
followed in turn
by sudden
opacity.

7.
It was not the evening of choice,
the theater with its smoky laughter
and maudlin tears.
The particolored curtain
chattering about free fall,
the subtext inscrutable.
The bogus dialogue
that charms bluestockings.
How they pore over
the program in search
of spiritual direction
or gossip or fashion advice.
A moment of darkness
relieves the gloom—

and then limelight
and blare and sulfur—
the pangs intensified,
the rabble uproarious.

8.
In the office
all is official,
files of light
cut corners
angular and true.
Each object holding
and withholding
the magic moment.
Scissors, paste,
typewriter. Above all
the telephone's insistent bell
with the power to summon him
to its court, no recourse.
Is there no way out,
is there no way—
the thought recurs
and is again cut short,
suppressed. Just like that
another day has fled.

9.
This is the room where hard sunlight
stakes its claim and darkens moods.
This is the book that confounds diligence.
Hard to read with the page so bright
and the air so still. This is the floor
that will not bear weight. Idly pull
a loose thread and now the plot unravels.
The pain that will not let go;
the dread that will not ease up.
This knife-edge of deep shadow
clarifying persistent doubts.

10.
Once again the backlog extends into evening,
all the columns that will not total out,
the correspondence nagging from the inbox.
Nothing alleviates the ambient lighting,
not the radio, not the snippets of small talk—
movie plots and one-day markdowns,
close-out pricing, starlet tells all.
Shooting the breeze as it enters the window
and shuffles the papers, the eight common
fallacies of the modern workplace
all on display in the décor, the attire,
the *mise en scène*. Somewhere beyond
this door a telephone is ringing and ringing.
Will there be an answer? Yes and no. No.

11.
It's a hard road into this place,
and a longer way out. The dark woods,
the lonely storefront, no one
to pump the gas. The moment
for resolution has passed.
Nothing to do but sit and wait
out the gloaming. A dog barks
in the distance. Raccoons scour garbage.
Even a shotgun blast would be welcome,
anything to disrupt the gloom.
The next milepost is unknown, far off,
and there won't be a soul for all the trouble.

12.
Motels are for taking stock,
the degradation of surface sheen.
Illuminated objects become a reminder
of the journey's faulty premise.
The window frames a landscape
of uncertainties, the map has more
questions than answers

about the road ahead. It has become
important to linger a moment
on this bed, ignoring for the time being
the suitcase's insistent claim.
The western sky, reflected in mirrors,
promises a hard spell of aimless wandering.
Stationery on the desktop. Inkwell and pen.
A lifeline, perhaps? But what
would a letter home say?
Who would be there to read it?

13.
Early morning, not yet seven, and already
a desolate atmosphere scarring
the town's main drag. Shuttered storefronts,
windblown trash. Obscured messages taped
to windowpanes. A lone walker on an errand.
What is his object? Medicine? Milk? The paper?
A dog answers his footsteps with desultory barks,
a gate creaks on its hinges. Doorways recede
deep into shadow, reluctant to let their secrets out.
Dawn without promise; light without glow.

14.
The doctor called it anxiety,
a book said dread. Her friend
shook her head: *Just a funk,
girl, ocean air's what you need.
You'll be right as rain, no time.*
Now she's looking out a window:
dunes, sea oats, blue horizon,
that same blunt feeling adrift
on the wind that tousles her hair.
Down on the beach a capsized boat,
screeching gulls. She wants to shed
her clothes and all constraint,
let sunlight warm her skin
but there's no warmth here,

the light strangely cold.
Fragments of a dream needle her,
and when she hears the words
Lucy, honey, what's wrong,
the prickling of her skin is more
than she can bear. There could be tears,
but there won't be tears, only a plea.
I must make a clean break, I must.

15.
All too abruptly daylight leaves the room.
His prospects for the next few hours:
not good. He's had a dream
but lost the content, whatever stirs
beyond the pane, teasing the edge
of darkness, doesn't want his prayers.
Even the air is nervous, charged,
his skin like paper at the cusp
of flame. All day it's been a slow burn.
He expects the earth to feel dead,
absolutely dead, despite the kinetic dance,
the electric particles, the flare
that startles these window highlights.
There's a ritualistic text—secret
wisdom—to explain this night surge
but the code is lost, the words amount
to nonsense, nothing more, even if
the sound is lovely enough to inspire faith.
Won't such clamor only be futile?
Won't expression quickly pall?
So it goes when the day dies and night
filters into the corridors, the rooms
where novices await insight.

16.
Drink, drank, drunk again—
the various conjugations
of the DTs. And now storms

in the offing, "Stormy Weather"
on the radio, droll cosmic joke.
Crabs on the boil, crustaceans
writhing in a murky sky.
A man gropes in the blue light
of a motel room, hand brushing
objects he can't identify.
Sand blows against the screen
of an unhinged door. The bottles
have all been emptied. Who?
When? Why? Somewhere
beyond vision, storm clouds
are tossing in their sleep.
The morning mirror reveals
a doped dreamer sloshing about,
the waterline knee-deep and rising.
In motel rooms across the island,
dead-end drummers crack open
liquor cases, admitting failure.
By now he, too, should know
the drill: it's well past time to make
his preparations for a monsoon season
too soon come, his last for sure.
He knows what to do but can't
bring himself to act. Stasis is absolute.

There it is, closer now: the sound,
the smell of the coming rain.

DOUBLE-A PITCHING CHANGE

Maybe a thousand fans in the ballpark tonight,
here for diversion, escape, baseball's illusion
of suspended time. But something else is in the air,
made manifest late in the game:
a sudden surge of dread,
the old anxiety revisiting,
a ghost taking over the grounds.

It's the top of the seventh, two on, no outs.
A graying veteran, former all-star in the bigs,
is scuffling in his comeback bid.
He's lost it, can't find the strike zone.
Ten straight balls—wide, high, in the dirt.
The radioman says home plate is
"jumping around on him."

The pitcher scoops some dirt, rubs the ball,
wipes a sleeve across his brow,
kicks into the rubber, squints toward home.

The baby-faced catcher, not long out of high school,
calls time and trots out to the mound,
ignorant of the cruel plot now unraveling,
blind to all omens: the noose in the grass
disguised as a groundskeeper's hose;
the dirge concealed in the organ's carnival tune;
the unexpected chill that has insinuated itself
into the air this midsummer's eve.

The pitcher digs and digs with his spiked shoes.
The catcher chews gum, spits, says nothing.

Now comes the manager's slow stroll,
head down, hands in back pockets
as he makes his way to take the ball

and, grim-faced, signal for relief.
After the game he will call the front office
to file his report recommending waivers.

"Just a shadow of his former self,"
the radioman says. "Sad to see."

The pitcher knows it: he's no longer
the ace, the go-to guy, the stopper.
He's washed up, in the lingo of the boys
leaning on the dugout railing, a has-been
about to leave the field for good.
This is it, the long, last walk,
ghost-escorted, from mound to dugout
before a scattered and indifferent crowd.

Pausing at the threshold, the pitcher
takes a final look around the ballpark.
The outfielders are stretching hamstrings,
pounding mitts, impatient to get on with it.
The mascot, freighted with a bulbous head,
reels along the catwalk, far gone in his cups.

Scorecard fanatics diligently cross out
the pitcher's name and pencil in his replacement.
In the bleachers a lone man repeats and repeats
a hapless gesture: jumping from his seat,
flinging arms above his head.

The pitcher gazes into the night sky
past the light standards, the humming sodium lamps,
the moths swimming in cigarette haze:
high in the purified twilight a shooting star flares
and burns out. He is the only one to see it.

At last he brings himself to look out to the bullpen
where the gate opens and a live-armed kid,
a promising prospect, comes sprinting
across the grass and dirt to take his place.

The old pitcher tips his cap
to desultory applause and apathetic jeers.
He descends the dugout steps, passes down
the row of silent, stone-faced teammates,
and crosses the threshold into darkness.

Then the tunnel, the locker room,
the cage he must clean out
before the final bus ride home.

CROSSING NEW MEXICO

First stop: Tucumcari, the main drag, old Route 66,
now a desolation row of ghost motels and neon motor courts
crouching in the shadow of a once-sacred mountain.
La Puerta—*Your Gateway to Heaven*;
Wagon Wheel—*Where the West Stops to Rest*;
Sky Court, Trade Winds, Sand and Sagebrush;
Pony Soldier, Buckaroo, Trailblazer, Apache, Zia.
The sixty-foot saguaro of the Cactus Court.
The Palomino's marvelous neon horse rearing
to the stars and neighing WHOA!—
answering with that flashing word
the day's most pressing question, posed
for a hundred miles on redundant billboards:
Why not, why not Tucumcari tonite?

***

Hungry? Take a break in Santa Rosa!
Grinning from a faded billboard,
a cartoon fat man offers friendly advice:
for the best in town, Club Cafe's the place to go.
World famous breakfast burritos.
Huevos rancheros, your choice of red or green.
Carne adovada swimming in a spicy sauce.
Puffy sopapillas oozing honey and hot oil.
Distinctive and Different since 1935,
the proof is in the fat man's grin.

***

Albuquerque, oh Albuquerque—plaintive refrain
to Neil Young's song, punchline to
a Looney Tunes gag—make no wrong turns in
Albuquerque, oh Albuquerque: where travelers
on old 66 were met with fiberglass jackrabbits,
giant arrows stuck in the ground,

a chieftain in headdress waving How!
Oh, oh, Albuquerque: derelict motels
down by the Rio Grande; boarded-up shops
and empty bars; ravens perched in cottonwoods.
"This part of town used to be something,"
the barkeep says, "in the days before the inner state."

Climbing the grade west of town,
smell of burning transmission oil.
Petroglyphs scratched onto boulders.
Defunct volcanoes poking from wasteland.
A series of tumbledown signs, barely legible,
leaning from the wind over a decaying roadbed:
>   *Rattlers Exit Now—*
>   *See 'em Live—*
>   *Free Snake Garden—*
>   *Live Poison Show—*
>   *Exotic Raptiles.*

***

Gassing up in Grants? Go with Gus!
Santa Fe Avenue, turn left three blocks.
Old Gus Chavez: veteran of foreign wars,
uranium miner, Esso man from way back.
Didn't want to change the sign to Exxon, no sir.
Keeps the old one in the boneyard out back.
Didn't want to switch out the pumps neither,
'cause them old Tokheim pumps were best,
never a problem. Got them stored out back, too.
Go take a look. Gus washes the windshield,
checks the oil, shows kids some baby rattlers in a box.
Same toy rattlers for thirty years, he laughs.
Out back, a rooster guards a boneyard
chockablock with porcelain thrones, coffins,
and assorted stone memorials: lyres, angels,
virgins, urns, crosses, obelisks. And beyond that,
a couple hundred rusted cars, glass

and enamel gone, doors caved in, chasses fallen
like a would-be soldier's weak arches.
They all come off old 66, Gus says: Falcons,
Fairlanes, Mavericks, Barracudas, Ramblers,
Mustangs, Skylarks, Impalas, Thunderbirds.
Cars that crashed, cars that gave up the ghost.
This here's their final resting place, Gus says
by way of farewell. You folks drive safe now,
buckle up them kids. Watch out for mule deer.

***

When in Gallup, trade at: Pow Wow Trading Post.
Trade for arrowheads, beaded belts, buffalo horns,
steer skulls, bullwhips, rubber snakes, shot glasses,
Zia key chains, made-in-China headdresses,
Route 66 placemats, 3-D images of Jesus
and Mary, Elvis and the Duke in black velvet.
And over here you've got your fool's gold,
geodes, Apache tears, mica shafts,
turquoise bracelets, thunderbird bolos,
dinosaur eggs, petrified wood, stuffed jackalopes,
mounted Gila monsters, scorpions under glass,
dancing kachinas, Navajo blankets, Zuni pots,
and postcards of the Land of Enchantment's most famous
relic: the blackened face of Jesus scorched onto a tortilla.

PASSING THROUGH

> *America is a poem in our eyes, its ample*
> *geography dazzles the imagination.*
> — Ralph Waldo Emerson

Abilene: Line cook taking a cigarette break outside the Hitching Post.

Browning: Lightning reveals Coyote, patient trickster, lurking by a dead tree.

Centralia: Headstones, angels, and urns in the showroom windows of Eternity Monuments.

Dickinson: *Just the miles of Stare—that signalize a Show's Retreat—in North America.*

Elko: Is this what death is like, a town of trash pickers, bored cashiers, insomniacs staring at the night wind?

Farmington: Radio relay towers on a ridge above a hardpan graveyard. Plastic flowers. Child's pinwheel spinning over a grave.

Galesburg: What's left when the long train passes? Windblown scraps tumbling, lifting, floating over the railbed.

Havre: Drifter sets down his bundle, drinks from a paper bag, does a little dance.

Iuka: Another warning sign—*Look up your redeemer draws near.*

Jellico: Three grackles mocking the First Baptist parking lot.

Kayenta: Shapeshifting clouds in all the colors of a Navajo rug—silver, turquoise, vermillion, charcoal.

Lander: Lone child squats in the sand of a horseshoe pit digging with a plastic shovel.

Madras: *Just a poor, wayfaring stranger traveling through this world below.*

Needles: Waking from a fever dream to blinding light.

Ocala: Downtown Diner, circle of elders holding hands in prayer before coffee and donuts.

Portage: Those men probing the drainage ditch, what are they looking for?

Quanah: Ravens surveilling sporadic traffic from the roof of a ramshackle filling station.

Red Rock: Prison crew in orange jumpsuits spearing roadside trash.

Sedalia: High beams catch an opossum sniffing the steps of a double-wide.

Tutwiler: *Going where the Southern cross the Yellow Dog.*

Umatilla: Two deputies standing over a sheeted corpse.

Vicksburg: *So foul a sky clears not without a storm.*

Weed: Waitress thinks the fox and her kits living under the dumpster out back must be some kind of omen, good or bad she can't say.

Xenia: Hostile traffic stop, static crackling on the sheriff's two-way.

Yucca Valley: The agonized shadow of a Joshua tree. *Oh, Lord, grant me vision, oh, Lord, grant me speed.*

Zapata: Borderlands, end of the road, liminality. Horseman on the riverbank staring at the other side.

I-10, WESTBOUND

In Deming, a dirty window
alters the color of the sky.

I sit in a diner drinking coffee,
parsing photos made in passing:
remnants of ranch houses, collapsed fences,
junkyards, the wreckage of a small plane
behind barbed wire on government land.

Signs and wonders here and there as I go.

I have an erratic car
no particular endpoint
and an old dog along for the ride.
Lordsburg and the border beckon.

One hundred miles on
I find an abandoned campground
pale rocks slipping
like lizards into sand.
Luminous bombers leave vapor trails
high above this so-called
land of enchantment.

Spilled oil makes a rainbow in water.
The dog sniffs the puddle beneath the car
but does not deign to drink.

Is there an end to this drifting?

Every horizon brings me
to a new domain and omens
of the impending crash.

| | two | |

HAIBUN: HITCHHIKING, FIRST RIDE

The first ride took me all the way to Montana, new territory for me, never having been farther east than Idaho. Bound for Butte, the drummer was pleasant at first but soon turned glum as he spoke of hard times and poor sales. "Never thought I'd end up like this," he said four or five times in a hundred miles. I looked out at horse pastures, pine forests, mountain streams, reservoirs and dams, convinced that I was right to leave, escape the dull routine, make a clean getaway. The known world ended at Coeur d'Alene. I remembered its main street from family outings at the lake, I knew its burgers and shakes, the IGA, the filling station where the drummer stopped for gas and a piss. Back on the road, he said, "Three hundred miles to go and after that who the hell knows." Then he fell silent and in silence we rode the rest of the way, coming into Butte at last under a sulfurous cloud, the gritty haze of mineral extraction. The drummer left me with a last word of advice: "Don't let anyone steer you wrong, kid. Stick to your guns. It's the only way you'll get by in this fucked-up world."

> *Far from home—now what?*
> *Lone prairie, sudden hailstorm*
> *a tree's poor shelter.*

STARLIGHT

Nightfall caught me on the edge
of some town; I no longer remember
its name or even the state,
but I do remember the movie complex—
the Starlite 8—and the open space
adjacent to the parking lot
with a little pond, shade trees, and a bench.
Good place to pass the night:
close to the highway but hidden,
little chance I'd be spotted or hassled
(the small-town cops being hard
on hitchers). I left my pack and bedroll
by a tree then sat a while on a grassy verge
looking up at the violet neon sign
lighting up one letter at a time.
S-T-A-R-L-I-T-E-8, the whole name
blinking three times before the spelling
exercise began again. Then the show let out.
A teenaged crowd spilled through the lot
where parents waited in cars. A few boys,
new to driving, jangled keys and smirked.
A young couple wandered my way
and I receded into shadow, like the wolf spider
I'd watched one day in a freeway rest area
as it dropped into its burrow each time
I dragged a stick nearby. They stood
close, silent for some time, and peered
into the pond. In a low voice he said,
"I just don't think we'll get away with it."
And she: "It's like the cartoon says,
it's so crazy it just might work."
For a while we listened to cars
driving off. Crickets filled the void.
Then he kissed the top of her head
saying, "All right, let's give it a try."

And they strolled back to the parking lot,
his hands in his pockets, her arms folded
across her chest, clutching herself.
Their footsteps faded. The neon marquee
went dark. Lying on the bench,
rucksack for a pillow, I watched Orion
the Hunter climb and cross the night sky,
blazing Sirius, the ever faithful
dog star, trailing at his heels.

HITCHHIKING AT NIGHT

It's a hard line to walk—midnight, full moon, high desert.
You're being questioned, but the nimbus has caught your eye.
What is it about omens and signs? They appear so often
in a moment of distraction when there's a more pressing concern.
You take in a general impression. But beyond that, what?
The details slip free, not to mention deeper meaning.
There's loose gravel under your feet, the smell of sage.
Distant lights of a radio relay tower.
The cop has stopped the interrogation to listen—
staticky news of a wreck somewhere on the highway ahead,
"possible fatalities." Then he's gone, and you are left alone,
free to wander, free to drift through the night under the eerie moon,
the nimbus that warns of something—a storm, a change in weather,
threats in a language you do not speak. Keep walking the line,
it's all you can do, cutting for sign, following the clues,
the sparkling trail of broken glass, the roadkill carcasses picked clean,
the residue of tumbleweeds atomized in the whirlwind.

PANTOUM: DOWN AND OUT

Back in there is where we camped, south of town
along the tracks leading from the switching yard.
You would think it's easy to jump a freight.
Not so. You need skill, know-how, good bit of luck.

Along the tracks leading from the switching yard
dangers abound; guards bring around bad dogs.
To dodge them you need skill, know-how, lots of luck.
You're sure to take a beating now and then.

Danger waits wherever you're bound—guards and dogs,
hunger and rain, drunken teens. You stay keen,
still you get a good beating now and then,
and it's time to move on down the line,

to more hunger, more rain, more drunk kids keen
to mock your misery. "Posted no vagrancy" means
the time has come to move on down the line,
jump a boxcar after the watchman passes.

Vagrancy means nothing but mockery, misery,
hiding out in wet bushes, a cold night. Wait until
the watchman passes, jump on board a boxcar
that bangs, skirls, lurches, then stalls on a sidetrack.

Back to the cold wet bushes, waiting all night,
thinking about coffee, thinking about dry shoes.
A sidetracked life of banging, skirling, lurching, stalling.
Helps to have comrades Bodie, Ringo, Utah Joe,

chatting about coffee, dry shoes, women, failure.
Nothing easy about jumping freight, the drifter's life.
You need comrades like Bodie, Ringo, Utah Joe.
Back in there is where we camped, south of town.

MANY DETOURS

I was stranded somewhere in Nebraska—I forget the town's name. A bitter cold day, a wind that brought tears. After two bootless hours at a filling station on the outskirts—telling drivers I was trying to get to Denver or anywhere in that direction—I walked into town along the frontage road, veering into a ditch (cracking through thin ice) whenever the big trucks roared past. Christmas decorations flapping at the used car lot. Pickup trucks parked at the Tack and Feed. Bus depot locked tight. Steam obscuring the diner's windows. I found the library by the post office, just off the courthouse square, and entered the warm reading room. Set down my pack, took a seat at a table, watched by the librarian and a handful of patrons. In their eyes, I was nothing but a drifter, a vagrant, a stranger in a town where there were no strangers. But they let me be, and for an hour I read the newspapers and magazines, feet and hands thawing. Through months of hardship on the road I had not kept up with the news and now I read about the president's intractable problem, the unending conflict overseas, the fall of governments in South America. There were communities perplexed by kidnappings and addiction. The weather confounded everyone. And what to make of the price of food? Of gasoline? Recent statistics disturbed officials, and in public opinion an ill wind blew. The nation furrowed its brow—never, the editorialists opined, had the impending holidays seemed so grim.

I finished reading and stared out the window. Flurries now, a heavy overcast sky. At any time I could call it off, put an end to this drifting, go back to Spokane, home, the people who waited for me—still angry, but ready to forgive, perhaps. I had no reason to believe things would go any better in Denver. Worse for all I knew. A warehouse, a slaughterhouse, gravel work. Busting my hump, paycheck to paycheck, barely getting by. Before I left the library for the bus depot, the librarian asked me to fill out a brief questionnaire. They were trying to keep the library open in the face of budget cuts. What had been the purpose of my visit? There was no obvious answer (other than "escape from the cold"), so I wrote the words that had haunted me since I first read them in high school—a catchphrase, a dictum, a mantra taken from Roethke's "Journey to the Interior":

*In the long journey
out of the self there are
many detours.*

ROAD KILL

In Tennessee I hitched a ride
and held the head of a deer
for a hundred miles.

***

On a Greyhound in Texas,
the carcass of a lamb,
hooves bound with baling wire,
occupied the seat across the aisle.

***

In the Caravan Motel,
the night manager apologized
for the mongoose laid out in the lobby,
a prized family pet, last link to their homeland.
"You can understand our grief," he said,
and invited me to view the silken shroud,
a gold and indigo fabric, richly lit
in candlelight, draped loosely
over banded fur.

***

Short on cash I took a job
with a traveling carnival
and sideshow zoo. First night out
the ringmaster detailed me to dispose
of a monkey that had suffered badly.
"Watch you don't touch them sores," he said
then threw open the door to the travel trailer.
I found the carcass in the shower stall
wrapped in a pink vinyl curtain.

The bearded lady moaned from the bed.
"He was a good little guy," she sobbed
while the Lobster Boy stroked her head.

ELK HERD

For all that happened that day—some of it the kind of brutality meant to leave a lasting impression—what I remember most is the herd of elk. The day began on some Colorado back road, the car dead. "No problem," Ray said. "We can hitch the rest of the way." "All the way to Vegas?" I said. "What about the car?" Ray shrugged. "Leave it." "Who's going to stop for two guys like us?" I asked. Ray just said what he always said. *No problem.* We walked along the highway for miles without luck. Then there was the country store on the outskirts of some town named Pistol or Gunshot. Ray wanted to get a pack of cigarettes, but when we counted out our change we came up short. "Well, shit," Ray said. "Ain't nothing but price-gougers in these two-bit towns." Ray's rolled-up sleeves and vivid baby-doll tattoos didn't help the cause. The clerk, an old guy working his gums, said nothing, just glowered straight at us until we scooped up the coins and left. We knew what would come next. Sure enough, not a mile down the road, the sheriff's deputy pulled alongside to administer a pop quiz, and he made it clear he didn't like our answers. Not one bit. Said our kind wasn't welcome in these parts. "Aw, Christ," Ray said. "It's a free country, ain't it?" In short order we were sitting cross-legged by the rear wheel of the cruiser, hands cuffed behind our backs, deputy's radio crackling as he called in an ID check. "Look at that," I said. Off in the pine woods, shadows were moving among the trees. "See the deer?" Ray squinted. "Not deer," he said. "Them are elk."

Ray fell back into a doze. I watched the elk as they slowly emerged from the trees to graze in open field, a couple of them staring cautiously at the men, the car, the flashing lights. It was amazing to see—their size, the antlers, their easy gait through the tallgrass, a grace unfamiliar to me. For the time being, transfixed, I forgot where I was. One elk seemed to return my gaze, watching intently as the deputy came around, stood over us with his billy club, and said, "Well now boys, how's about we take a little ride?"

HITCHHIKER'S NIGHTMARE

It's the hitchhiker's worst nightmare:
waiting on the shoulder for a ride
when the Law comes skidding.
Get a move on pal, your kind ain't wanted here.
So on you go, trudging toward the outskirts.
But the cop comes back before you get a mile down the road.
Guess you didn't get the message, pal.
You hard of hearing or just thick in the head?
If it's one thing you've learned, there's nothing
a hitcher can do when the Law wants to bust your ass.
Next thing you know you're spread-eagle
against the cold metal of the cruiser, teeth smashed into the hood.
One swift kick sends you down into a snow-filled ditch.

Middle of the night and you're still walking the lost highway,
too cold to bed down. Stupor and chill, stupor and chill—
you feel it in brain and bones. When headlamps crop up,
you crouch in tallgrass, you slink behind signposts.
Ghost owls watch from darkened trees.
But in Hassle County you can only get so far. You know
what's coming over the horizon: Can't evade it, pal,
can't dodge it, can't get away, not this time, not ever.
Sure enough, here's the wailing siren, the spinning blue and red lights,
the highway patrol on the prowl for someone answering your
    description.
The searchlight flares, and he's got you dead to rights.

CROSSING FLAGSTAFF

Snow fell the morning I trudged into Flagstaff.
Snow on snow, more snow than I had ever seen.
Storefronts banked with snow. Empty streets.
There must be some place open up ahead,
I thought—diner, tavern, railway depot.
But no, nothing, the whole town shuttered tight.
Icicles daggered down from the depot's eaves,
and a murder of crows studied me
from window wells when I paused.
Move on, they cawed, *move on*.
Shrewd advice. I took it to heart
and pressed on blindly into
a hard wind and whiteout.

I came upon the hobo camp,
now buried and deserted,
wiser vagrants than I having
skipped town for the season.
Knee-deep, trying to read
the ice-glazed signs, I understood:
This is how it will be.
Snow will fall and go on falling,
and I will keep on keeping on,
crossing one snowbound town
after another, kicking through drifts
the length of my days.

POEM GOING NOWHERE

Facing the blank page: it's like long days spent hitchhiking.
You're just waiting for a ride to come along,
the vehicle that can take you somewhere, anywhere.
Fast, slow, east, west: it really doesn't matter.
After a few hot hours roadside you'll go anywhere.
Drug-addled hipster in a rundown van? *Doesn't matter.*
Bible salesman tripping to gospel radio? *Doesn't matter.*
Crazy dude pushing conspiracy theories? *All right, whatever.*
Drunken war stories, crash-and-burn melodrama,
accounts of alien abduction, testimony about finding God in
    prison:
You'll sign on for the ride, you'll listen up good.
The trickster who plays on your gullibility then scoffs—
"Don't believe that shit, just pulling your leg, bro"—
you'll take the bait, you'll play the fool
so long as it gets you started.
Good ride, bad ride—doesn't matter.
Any ride's better than no ride.

And here is a station wagon prowling past, vintage model
chock full of junk, glare on the cracked glass,
rusted door held shut with twine, wheels out of balance,
chassis riding low. He's slowing down,
pulling to the verge thirty yards ahead, little cloud of dust.
This is it, your chance at last: you shoulder the pack,
trot along the gravel, grateful, eager to get going.
And just when you're drawing near, the bastard
hits the gas and roars off, spewing rocks and dirt,
leaving you in a rut, ever and always at a standstill.

| | three | |

VARIATIONS ON FIVE PHRASES FROM SUSAN SONTAG

1. *Intellectual Vertigo*
Think about it deeply but don't look down.
You're well into the third treatise
when you realize there's no guardrail
and any mishap could lead
to a long, long plunge.

2. *Tortured Spiritual Impulse*
Would be better some days
to stay in bed, sleep it off
with Valium or whatever
does the trick. But no,
you're wide-awake,
standing at the window,
watching a lightning storm.

3. *Willed Derangement*
Rejections come in quick succession,
criticism ranging from mild
to frankly vitriolic.
The logical response: forego
all attempts to impose order.
House a cluttered mess,
clothes in disarray, speech
devolving into non-sequiturs.

4. *Self-imposed Exile*
The injunction appears in the fine print.
You have it from the highest authorities,
and appeals are now exhausted.
Here is what the ghost owl says
in the middle of the night:
Go. Go now.

5. *Compulsive Travel*
The itinerary no longer serves a purpose.
Names on the destination board flip past.
Movement is all that matters,
an overwhelming urge to postpone arrival.
Here's a sidetrack, an inscrutable map,
one more chance for divergence,
a change of skies, a clean break.

EN ROUTE: APALACHICOLA, FLORIDA

On the road into town we keep an eye
out for osprey nests, marveling at
their construction atop telephone poles.
The anhingas, too, are a wonder,
airing their wings as they perch
on posts along the waterfront.

Strolling the streets of Apalachicola,
we come across families on holiday,
kids licking ice cream cones, public meltdowns,
quarrels about where to go next,
what to do in the tedious hours ahead.

In the Oyster City Bar, someone's laughing
about a bad sunburn: "You should've seen
the top of his head. Like a big, fat tomato!"
Rank sea tang permeates everything,
the Gulf Coast in July. In the park, a statue:
Doctor Gorrie, inventor of air conditioning.

There's something still unresolved,
something left unsaid, the quandary
we've brought with us but refuse to confront.
We stare at the offing, the buildup
of storm clouds bringing to mind Emerson:

When we look at ourselves in the light of thought,
we discover life is embosomed in beauty,
all things assuming pleasing forms, as clouds do far-off.

THREE THOUSAND MILES: A HAIBUN SEQUENCE

> *I felt three thousand miles rushing through
> my heart, the whole world only a dream.*
> — Bashō, *The Narrow Road*

1. *Terre Haute*

Indiana: a week of artificial illumination, the sky constantly overcast, persistently gray. Not the interesting dark gray of stormy skies, the kind of gray that lends itself to brooding art (think Friedrich, think Turner). Just the uniform, pallid gray of Indiana in winter. A week spent mostly indoors, shuttling among fluorescent rooms, hardly a breath of fresh air, one overly gregarious event after another. Wine and cheese, platters of chilled shrimp, tiramisu in Dixie cups. Perfunctory questions about authorial intention and poetic license, enthusiastic anecdotes about family trips to Branson, Orlando, Vegas. So went our week in Terre Haute: no chance of natural light, no escape from polite conversation, no way to avoid the constant expressions of concern about the performance of the local basketball team. "I'll tell you what," someone said. "You've got that right. Hit the proverbial nail right on the head." Three different people at three different events quipped, "Once a Hoosier, always a Hoosier." They all had big grins, booming voices. In the hotel's breakfast nook, the same grin, same voice emanated from a television screen: "Look for more of the same tomorrow, folks. Overcast skies, highs in the upper thirties."

> *That seasick feeling,*
> *hotel corridor at night.*
> *Too much chardonnay.*

2. *Carbondale*

Three days in Carbondale exhausted our philosophical inclinations. In the pancake house, we stared at bowls of congealed oatmeal and failed to get the powder to dissolve in cups of tepid coffee. It was obvious we were teetering toward ennui and must soon get out of town. Nevertheless, there was one more interview and a museum to visit before we were allowed a clean getaway. Non sequiturs abounded: the waitress's running commentary on the shortage of help in the kitchen; the committee's off-base queries about samizdat poetry in Eastern Europe; the museum displays on gopher holes and the long, underappreciated history of sackcloth attire. A man on the corner of Cherry and Ash ate from a paper bag and singled us out to say: "This is the best damn donut I ever ate, bar none."

This storefront window:
silk orchids, pastel-colored;
a dozing tabby.

3. Davenport

In Davenport, the hopeless interview took place in a glass and steel box. Bagels and coffee were delivered, bagels in a box, coffee in a box. There was some grousing about the fact that once again the delivery did not include French vanilla creamer. "Our first question," the chairperson said, "has to do with your methodology, because it's not all that clear—right?—how you've reached these conclusions." Hours passed before we were released and could go for an assuasive walk in a nearby park—uplifted somewhat to see trees that had budded in defiance of the cold wind, the slush on the walkways. We shivered in our inadequate jackets; we rued the answers we had given to the committee's cleverly phrased questions—designed, we realized, to catch us out, expose an untenable position. We already knew we would have to count Davenport among our losses, but somehow seeing those buds—little furry green nubbins on bare branches—made everything better. "Long run, things will turn out for the best," we decided as we gingerly negotiated the ice-choked puddles, the wind pushing hard against us. "All shall be well, and all shall be well, et cetera, et cetera."

> *Late winter, cold wind,*
> *the park pond still thick with slush.*
> *Children feeding geese.*

4. *Lincoln*

In Lincoln, it was decided that we should see the football stadium and the statehouse then go out for steak. Our hosts—affable to a fault—chatted from the front seat as they drove us around town. We circled the stadium. We circled the statehouse. I noticed the trees (ash?), the clouds (high cirrus?), and the flags—so many flags—adorning houses. At the steakhouse, enormous slabs of meat were set before us. Biscuits. Corn on the cob. Our hosts poured on the steak sauce and asked scores of questions that seemed irrelevant, off topic. The place was loud with talk about football even though football season was months off. Everybody wore red. The walls were decorated with sports memorabilia. I asked one of our hosts about Red Cloud, Willa Cather's hometown. She had never been but had heard it was nice. Well, not nice exactly but interesting. The drive to get there, she said, was dull, dull, dull.

> *Morning without warmth,*
> *a mug of tasteless coffee.*
> *This endless journey.*

5. *Beaumont*

What was it the committee chair wanted us to see out his office window? Something just below, three stories down near the building's entrance. Was it a rose garden? A peculiar piece of modern sculpture? A bike rack? What we noticed—couldn't help but notice—was the refinery just across the way, the array of storage tanks. "You get used to them," he told us. "Like telephone poles. You don't see them after a while." Our presentation was poorly attended, and those in the room projected a practiced apathy. There were no questions. Conflict with a sporting event of some sort, the committee chair explained.

Or was it the start of hunting season? Whatever, we shrugged it off, having become inured to sparse and weary audiences. Then it was lunch at a sandwich shop, the chair wolfing down enormous bites of roast beef and telling us all about his research. He seemed surprised we weren't familiar with a certain study to which he had contributed. There was no finishing the hefty, bland sandwiches. The smell of petroleum was everywhere, and everything—bread, water, meat—tasted of chemicals.

> *Beyond city sprawl—*
> *transformers, tank farms, train tracks.*
> *Then: wetlands in mist.*

6. *Durango*

A cloudless day in Durango; fresh, cool, autumnal air; warm sunlight. Nonetheless, the riveting news was of a hurricane thousands of miles away. Disastrous flooding. People and pets on rooftops. Boats navigating inundated streets. An ineffectual government response, the military mobilized. Everywhere—in the hotel lobby, the student center on campus, the sports bar—screens replayed footage of storm surge, fallen trees, downed wires, collapsed structures, flipped mobile homes, confused and dazed victims. But when we walked outside, strolled the grounds, watched the Frisbee-tossers and dogwalkers, we found ourselves in a carefree world, an Indian summer day, making it easy to pretend that all the inclemency was elsewhere, that we ourselves could remain blissfully unaware of our own impending storms.

> *Winding mountain roads,*
> *the map at odds with our route.*
> *Which way is true west?*

7. Fresno

Fresno was a mistake from the get-go, but who was to blame? A discussion of ultimate responsibility proved overly intricate and finally bogged down on conflicting versions of some nuance that may or may not have originated with Nietzsche. Besides, it was hard to breathe: swirling dust, diesel exhaust, a persistent agricultural haze burning the throat. Three sad palms, discolored from the bad air, governed the motel parking lot. No one from the state university came to meet us (a combination of miscommunication and overbooking at the campus day-care facility, according to the terse explanation we later received). And so we undertook the long walk up the main boulevard straight toward the epicenter of the California nightmare—six lanes of traffic, drive-thru fast food, auto trader, smoke shop, nail salon, bowling alley, cineplex, orthodontics, pet hospital, memory care, car wash, military supplies, parking garage, extended-stay motel, finally an impassable cloverleaf exchange—the nightmare that has unnerved many a revenant pilgrim from Henry James to Henry Miller. Outsiders, too: Brecht, Huxley, Adorno, Baudrillard. None made it so far as Fresno, but they knew the gist of it, having envisioned the grotesque American stylings of the wrath to come. Somewhere up ahead, we would find ourselves at the end of the road, contemplating the "many detours" that one meets, according to Roethke, on the long journey out of the self.

> *Now the deciding point.*
> *At the crossroads, haze confounds*
> *all sense of bearing.*

8. Chico

In Chico, we were put up in a room across from the dorms, a party in progress. Howls. Loud music. Hooting. "Oh my god that is so random," someone squealed. Hyena laughter. We reviewed our notes for the presentation and decided to cut the more controversial points, leaving only an innocuous argument intact. Hardly worth going through the motions to deliver it, but we had tired of the sophistries we continually met with in Q & A. Later, at the reception, we were introduced as "the guest speakers" to three retired members of the department, one of whom peered at us and said, "Ah yes, fine talk. I was sorry to have missed it." He directed our attention to a tray of cookies and named them for us: "Oatmeal, peanut butter, chocolate chip, and I don't know what these blonde jobs are—snickerdoodles, perhaps?" He stroked his gray goatee and pondered the enigma. It felt like we had arrived at some sort of an ending, nothing more to say, nowhere else to go beyond Chico except another Chico and another Chico after that, an endless string of Chicos, one after another, until the road petered out altogether.

nightfall, brooding trees
the auguries of ghost owls
a narrowing road

VARIATIONS ON A THEME FROM *NORTH BY NORTHWEST*

> *"Funny, that plane's dusting crops*
> *where there ain't no crops."*

Maybe it's the idea that terror can come of a sudden
dropping from an empty sky—and not at random but
with you and only you as target. Look: here it comes.

This is fate's way. The machine has caught you out.
The matrix keeps track wherever you run. Nice try, but
you cannot hide: the pilot has you always in sights.

The long shot ought to establish your insignificance;
it really shouldn't matter if you come or go, but
for reasons unexplained, you've been singled out.

The signs drift across the sky—shapeshifting, ambiguous.
From your vantage the messages signal nothing but
an advértisement for laundry soap. How cunning!

One day, you'll roam free with total abandon—a man
unencumbered wandering the open range, but
just now you're sprawled on your belly, clutching soil.

Add it up—the total always comes out one short.
All along you thought you had gone under the radar, but
now it seems these imponderables are homing in.

It's true: the airplane's dusting where there are no crops
and it's the moment of epiphany when the scales fall.
Over and over they told you bygones were forgotten, but
here's the swooping whirligig bringing in revenge.

POSTMODERN WESTERN

The establishing shot projects our peril:
this ends badly. Maybe even worse than expected.
A plotline like this has a way of slipping bounds.
So it goes when the moral arc bends
toward betrayal. All hell busts loose.
The backdrop: perfect Western weather—ominous,
the elements for disaster clicking neatly together.
Witness the atomic glow charging the sky,
the murder of crows roosting in a dead tree,
the deputy, the trickster, the harlot,
and yes, of course, the wise old shaman—
they all appear on cue and in their assigned places.
The soundtrack: a doleful harmonica.
Even now, the extrajudicial posse
is spinning fortune's wheel,
revving engines, calling for reinforcements.
Everything serves the rising action, the baleful mood:
the sun's glare, the heat mirage in a waterless land,
the melodramatic strumming of a Spanish guitar,
the crack of bullwhips, those cinematic Indians
lurking behind mesquite.

When does mere menace ever suffice?
Shouldn't we assume something still more
malevolent when the sun drops down? Hell, yes:
Cold-blooded fury comes galloping into town.
Red horse, red rider, dangling noose.
The player piano announces the theme
and then explodes, the hero on his knees in sawdust,
wiping blood from his mouth while the deputy grins:
"Looks like we got ourselves a slow learner."

Now the wild punch thrown in anger: as always,
a futile gesture, the kind that triggers payback,
the spinning chamber, the metallic click

of *vengeance is mine*, vultures keenly observing
the pileup of bulleted corpses—bandidos
who pushed class warfare past the point of no return.
One by one the hero's options are eliminated,
and any positive outcome requires a quicksand trail
down a box canyon, redemption granted
but never forgiveness, never absolution.
A hero is a hero only by going to Hell.

Does it in fact end badly? Damn straight it does.
For everyone involved and any number
of innocents as well: An overwhelming catharsis,
gale force, impelling our tumbleweed souls.

ANOTHER BAD DAY AT BLACK ROCK

for Richard Hugo

Ask yourself what brought you here,
this desert town at the end of washboard.
Not just what road but the backstory, too.
By now you should have conned it
never mind the amnesiac tendencies.
You've never been here before, not even close,
yet you feel like a revenant. Instant familiarity
without the dirty secrets.
The door to the bar is propped open,
blues on the jukebox. Go in, take a stool.
Ned will pour you the usual. Downwind:
the junk car graveyard smelling of lost innocence,
the drugstore always lacking the right medicine.
The one bend in the road is lined with crosses.
In the motel parking lot, the sheriff's deputy
arrives with lights flashing, something covered
with a sheet in the threshold to number seven,
the air like gasoline on the skin.
Schoolboys stand around smoking cigarettes.
Red Harrison's horse trots down Main.
An argument reaches fever pitch
in what you take to be Basque.
In the filling station, a long story
about a missing child is searching for closure.
A rifle pokes from an upstairs window.
A hand materializes to lower the shade.
The courthouse clock is stuck on eight-thirty.
Face it. This fugue state has left you
bewildered, a vague notion that someone
is tracking you down. And when the words
"Bad Day at Black Rock" appear on the marquee
of the boarded-up Bijou, you know
it's your call to action, the cue to do something,

at first you can't recall what. Then it hits you:
the awful task, the inescapable ordeal
that has lured you here and still lurks
somewhere down the dusty street.

EN ROUTE: CARRIZOZO, NEW MEXICO

We followed Billy the Kid's trail from Lincoln over to Carrizozo, listening as we went to old-time gospel radio, the only clear signal. *Farther Along. I Saw the Light. Precious Memories.* Historical markers recounted the outlaw's cruel encounters and narrow escapes, a land of gunfights, double-crosses, ambush. Reading the signs, we could hear a cold-blooded sneer in the wind.

Carrizozo: a town named for the native scrub grass, just plentiful enough to allow for high-desert cattle grazing. The pasturage attracted nineteenth-century ranchers, who came and took possession of the land, forcing the Antelope People to retreat to a mountain fastness. Then the railroad arrived, hailing Progress. Eventually, theorists and technicians found their way to the heart of the desert and carted in their secret plutonium core. Carrizozo trembled with the subsequent explosion, and the townspeople saw the first-ever mushroom cloud swell and descend.

We parked and walked along Highway 54 in search of a market, passing a quaint building which we took to be the library. Its small adobe façade evoked art deco, and a message was engraved over its threshold—a noble sentiment expressed in incongruous spelling: "The fountain of wisdom flows thru books."

It was a warm September morning. We found the market. In the adjacent lot, chiles were roasting, the pods tumbling in a screen drum hand-cranked over a gas flame, piquant smoke wafting over us as we watched. Inside the market, we found homemade burritos, the handiwork of a local *señora*, bought two for our picnic, and headed over to the state park, the Valley of Fires. We followed the twisting boardwalk through the lava beds, arguing all the while in detail about something trivial.

Then the silent drive straight toward the setting sun and a motel room in Socorro, one of the gospel songs stuck fast in my head: *Farther along, we'll know all about it, farther along, we'll understand why.*

UNCLE JACK'S WAR WOUND

Shortly after Parker's grisly death,
Jack went on furlough to the Philippines.
During war, things just happened, no use
asking how one moment led to the next.
It was all totally, brutally random, and that
was that. One day chance has Parker sit down
next to Jack in the mess tent. Small talk
turns up things in common. Stock car racing,
Bama football, Johnny Cash. Couple of
red dirt farm boys pulling jungle duty.
So they say, hey let's hang out some more,
maybe do something together next furlough.
Not twelve hours later, Parker's gone.
Accident. Mishandled mine. Blown to bits.
And Jack ends up strolling alone
down a stinking street in Olongapo.
The place was crazy with flies and girls,
very young girls standing in doorways,
hanging out windows, waving, whistling,
making these wacko sucking sounds.
At a sidewalk café, Jack sat for hours
over beer watching it all and contemplating
Parker's fate—casket in a cargo hold,
smartly trimmed plot in the Punchbowl.
The statue of a Catholic saint, gravely wounded,
wavered in the hot breeze. Coals glowed
in braziers and sent up coils of smoke.
The beer went flat and Jack, absorbed
in the city's stinks, watched an old woman
pushing a fish cart, the pile of gray fish
clouded with flies. Blood trickled from mouths.
Blood smeared the fishmonger's apron.
Jack didn't move, not even when the sky
darkened and brought on a downpour, rain
blowing hard into shops, the shopkeepers

hurriedly dropping plastic sheets
over their wares, lowering awnings.
Rickshaws scurried for cover, girls vanished into
bars and makeshift bedrooms, stray dogs
whimpered for shelter. It was all helter-
skelter but Jack sat on, mesmerized.
His glass of beer filled with rainwater and ran over,
and the gutters were raging with runoff
that had strangely turned a deep, deep red.
It was then he knew he'd never make it through,
and if there was a way—any way at all—
he had to get out of this goddamn war,
whatever it took, whatever it took.

UNCLE JOE, AWOL IN BANGKOK

Come down, come down—down to the dens, a riverine slum where courier kids kick at bones. Let the smell guide you to a stilted hut, clacking abacus, tar-stained fingers flipping through yellow banknotes, pipes laid out on a tray. Incense pours from joss sticks, an ontological haze, the warping of time. Deep breathing means the danger of memory: white phosphorus descending in clouds, jungle meltdown, villages in flames, the chaplain reciting psalms. White noise, white noise. The night lights of the tourist district spinning out of control. What has happened to the heart? Let's make a mockery of existential dread, puncture wounds tracking veins. In the parallel world, a house rat has chewed the *farang*'s shoe and left a fist-sized hole. A delusion? But you are wide-awake, alert, speeding through spacetime. You can see for yourself the elegant solution: you are caught in a quantum superposition—alive, dead; both, neither.

EN ROUTE: BEATTY, NEVADA

We bypassed Vegas and took the road up to Beatty, one hundred or so miles of bleak terrain: proving grounds of the hydrogen bomb, storage site of nuclear waste. Fighter jets in training crisscrossed overhead. "In every landscape," Emerson said, "the point of astonishment is the meeting of sky and earth." We drove on at seventy, eighty, ninety miles per hour, seemingly getting nowhere, the point of astonishment ever receding.

Then abruptly we hit Beatty, darkness descending. We called it a day, took a room at the Atomic Motel, a cluster of huddled bungalows with a torpedo stuck in a rock out front and wild burros roaming the dusty lot, sniffing at the metal figures of two-dimensional space aliens (some pink, some lime green) propped up here and there on the grounds.

A walk after dark brought us to the Stagecoach Casino squatting amid contorted, wind-bent desert palms, the spokes of its neon wagon-wheel sign giving the illusion of motion, Beatty's ever-turning wheel of misfortune. Inside, the Stagecoach was a dismal joint despite the upbeat cacophony and razzle-dazzle electronics. It soon wore us down, so we headed over to the Happy Burro for bowls of chili and lite beer in plastic cups. Back at the Atomic Motel, you wrote a letter and I closed my eyes to the uncanny wallpaper, the cartoonish western art hanging above the bed. All night long, something scratched inside the walls.

Come morning, the temperature already pushing ninety degrees, we went for the breakfast special at the local diner and confronted the basic fact of Beatty: it's a crossroads town and there are choices to make. Continue north to Reno, the same glitz and glimmer as Vegas, albeit on a smaller scale? Head east into the heart of the Great Basin, America's largest desert, with its thousand-year-old trees and sky islands? Or veer west to the ghost town of Rhyolite and a steep drop down into Death

Valley? Which direction should we choose?

Flies buzzed, a fan sputtered overhead. We studied the map. The toast was dry, the coffee bitter. We didn't know it yet, but in truth there was no choice. Possibilities, yes. Possibilities, but no real choice.

GHOST TOWNS OUT WEST

> *Many Western towns never lasted a single human lifetime.*
> — Wallace Stegner

Deadwood: Three times inside a year the place burned to the ground.

Radium Springs: Everyone went batty from a steady pinging sound.

Bullet Hole: The gunshots sang out night and day.

Quarryville: Before long wolves swooped in and had their way.

Mesquite Junction: The constant wind wiped out connecting roads.

Blighton: Fragmentary annals hint at vipers, locusts, toads.

Paradise Valley: They ate of the fruit—and bore God's wrath.

Sweetwater: They found artesian wells but forgot to do the math.

Fort Custer: Neither prayer nor cannon could stop the roving bands.

Arabia: Thus saith the Lord, *Do not build on shifting sands*.

Angel Fire: The good citizens began hearing voices.

Freewill: From start to end, they made bad choices.

Bonanza: A worthless claim—everyone was fleeced.

Rocky Ridge: From day one the tremors never ceased.

Wheatland: A scourge of root rot brought on its death knell.

Furnace Creek: The cartographers warned: Here be hell.

THE DONNER PASS DINER

You're always welcome at
the Donner Pass Diner
where friendly is our motto,
good food, too,
Truckee exit, turn left. One mile.

Palm resting on the Kiwanis gumball machine,
Pete Grigorian, Armenian refugee,
stands at the glass door and watches cars pass
his diner for the McDonald's down the road.
While patties sizzle on the grill,
Pete talks about history, not the history
that led him to flee his homeland, but local history,
the Donner party, snowbound pioneers
who once upon a time cannibalized their kin.
The lake upside the freeway bears their name,
a pretty shoreline ringed with pines.
Not many stop to look. They drive too fast,
miss the moral of the marker, the plaque
commemorating the hard-luck story: Caught
by early snows a mile from the pass,
made to endure the harshest and longest winter
on record, the Donners wasted away
until forced to gnaw the flesh of their dead,
America's great cautionary tale.

Over the years, Pete has decorated his diner
with Donner memorabilia, some of it displayed
in a vitrine where pies should be: tin cups,
wooden spoons, a crude knife fashioned from bone,
odd bits of calico and leather, one old boot.
A battered wagon wheel hangs from the ceiling.
Pete has gathered these relics during years
of digging and spading up at the lake,
hunting for Donner artifacts his great hobby.
In the supply room, he pulls the string on a dim bulb

to reveal stacks of boxes: Solo cups, catsup packets,
sacks of potatoes, onions, rice. And there in the middle:
a crate of bones—pelvis, femur, jaw. Whose?
Who knows. He dug them from muck near the lake.

Pete sets down a bone then from a sack takes up a potato
black and rancid with mold. "Think about it," he says.
"What they would have given to find this spud."

To those who listen long enough, Pete gives
a free bag of doughnuts, coffee to go.
Stop at the state park, he advises, a pretty place
he likes to go on Sundays when the sun shines warm
and the road melts free of snow. He stands now
at the diner window, watches patrons drive away,
turns his eyes to the mountains, the swirling snow,
the ghosts in the woods to whom on winter days
he leaves offerings of food and drink.

BIRTHPLACE

I no longer recall whose birthplace it was
we happened upon that day passing through
yet another dying American town,
the old house carefully restored,
tidily kept, and wholly without visitors
for weeks at a time to judge from the gaps
in the guest registrar. Once renowned,
his name known throughout the land,
he had long since lost relevance,
his day and time having come and gone,
such that even the most ardent student
of history now would shrug in ignorance.
Secretary of State for some minor president?
Inventor of a gadget long outmoded?
Writer of sentimental romances? General
in a war we'd rather forget? His erstwhile
claim to fame slipped my mind soon
after the place vanished in our rearview.

We pondered whitewashed floorboards,
cloudy antique mirrors, chiffoniers,
an iron bed with homespun quilts,
a room decorated for holiday cheer,
a writing desk behind velvet rope.
The docent told the story of a contented life
abruptly curtailed. Success and happiness
yielded to plague, infant death, mental illness,
the hardships of war. The once-astute mind
bent itself adroitly to financial ruin,
an impoverished death, eventual obscurity.
We wandered from room to room
admiring gaudy wallpaper, porcelain urns,
plates from Delft; then, tour over, exited

through a smart little gift shop that held out hope someone would buy postcards, t-shirts, mugs blazoned with a name that now meant nothing.

JOHN BERRYMAN, ENCYCLOPEDIA SALESMAN

In desperation he took the only job he could find: selling encyclopedias door-to-door.... By the end of the second day, without having placed a single order, 'trembling & half-mad,' he quit in disgust. — Paul Mariani, *Dream Song: The Life of John Berryman*

Rumpled and feckless, slumped
among dutiful commuters in smart suits,
John Berryman rides the crosstown train.
His remit: peddling encyclopedias door to door.

Oh, how his mood sours upon arrival,
the moment of silent clamor before
doors release and weighty bodies press
for expulsion. Now the platform,
now the turnstile, now the stairwell
echoing with a blind busker's blues
as he ascends to an avenue
bustling with commercial purpose.

What's he doing here,
wasting his time, trembling
and half-mad amid
the droning procession?

Can he really bear one more
tenement day wandering
the poorly lit warrens wherein
dim-witted doors open
to the smell of bacon grease
and backed-up plumbing?
His sales pitch—an elegant quatrain—
avails him nothing.

Better to malinger, shirk the charade,
celebrate the day's seizure. Henceforth,
nothing—nothing—must forestall
the ardent singing of his dreams.

LAND OF OPPORTUNITY

Factory noise follows him wherever
he goes, a buzz in his head long after
the safety suits are hung up for the night
and the timeclock has stamped his card.
The coffee shop waitress says something
and he just nods, always at a loss,
the harsh language, the constant buzz in his head
keeping him from understanding the here and now.
The waitress brings him unwanted bread—
bland American bread, which he did not ask for
and does not like. Every day goes like this:
work, misunderstandings, food without flavor,
more work. Letters from home worry
how he will cope with winter weather.
But when the season comes he just feels numb,
too numb to register the cold,
and even his sorrow, his longing,
succumb to the numbness of routine:
train to work, safety suit, foul air,
mechanical noise, hoses, belts, gauges,
train back to the shared flat. Day in, day out.

Sometimes on the train the police scrutinize him.
Or a passenger stares intently with hateful eyes.
How tiring to always, always be suspected.
Night falls too early here. He travels through corridors
of wan light—the tenement buildings' pallid squares,
the pale-yellow underground stations. His own ghost
rides alongside him in the pane, and beyond his phantom face
are vacant lots, railroad yards, housing projects,
and people fixed in place on shadowy platforms.
Bulky, sober clothing. Frozen faces. Nothing like
the glittering America he saw in movies long ago, mesmerized
in his hometown's sweltering makeshift theater.

When with the train's sway he dozes,
he's transported to the carnival dances he knew as a boy,
his family—mother, father, grandparents,
cousins, uncles, aunts—in animal masks
weaving around him until he is subsumed,
trampled in the confused quadrille.

Jarred awake by the lurching train, he finds
he has missed his stop and must descend
to a strange sector harboring some other
foreign enclave, the language, the street patterns,
the stores and their products all strange to him.
A coppery prostitute has him by the arm,
her accent too severe for him to follow.
When he can't answer her question,
she scoffs and shoves him away.
Someone down the block shouts at him,
and he turns a corner, finds a shadow, turns
and turns again. After an hour of wandering,
penniless, he enters a tunnel under tracks
and hurries through: the reek of urine and liquor,
violent threats graffitied on the walls,
the blasting of train horns, gun shots,
and then at last the neighborhood he knows,
a street he recognizes, storefronts lettered
in his native tongue, familiar displays,
the trappings of his homeland weirdly
manifesting here, in this foul and frigid city,
his exile, his nightmare, his last-ditch hope.

UNCLE JERRY, MISSING IN ACTION

He's riding a motorcycle out of bounds,
a man on a mission, advancing at a slow crawl
over and around elephant holes
toward the inevitable roadblock,
going just fast enough for the stirred air
to bring tears to his eyes behind sunglasses.
Insects glance off his head and chest.
Engine noise—putter and cackle of the two-stroke—
drowns out excited chatter about his passage.
Old men understand: he embodies an omen.
Girls avert eyes from the unlucky avatar.
He's trying to find his way, but road signs
are hopelessly convoluted, the strange
alphabet impossible to decipher.
Every convergence and divergence, every fork
means guesswork. This or that road might lead
to fog bank, mountain barrier, impassable river,
opium hut in an uncharted village. On and on
he goes, quarreling with the road map,
pursuing its misdirections through hamlets,
paddies, quarries, napalmed forest.
Children and dogs race alongside yelling, barking,
pulling up of a sudden at unseen boundaries
as if to say, *Where are you going? That way is darkness.*
He's gone, long gone, checking the phrasebook
for tripwire and booby trap, a ghost that will haunt
the rainforest long after the rasping whirligig
forgets its imperial ambitions and takes flight.

REAGANOMICS: A MEMOIR

The news in those days was all about the coming plague, road rage,
    postal shooters.
Junk bonds were trending. Flag-burning triggered outrage, a crescendo
    of tub-thumping.
Inquiring minds wanted to know the intimate details of celebrity.
A heat wave settled on the heartland, pavement buckled, farms failed.
Ten million cicadas emerged from middle earth and took over the trees,
nonstop noise about trickle down and welfare queens.
Heavy metal misogyny. Wacko Jacko with a chimpanzee. The politics of
Piss Christ.

Everything was contra this and contra that. Strummer was bored with
    the USA
and Coltrane jammed on *Giant Steps* until the apartment next door
    banged on the wall
and yelled *turn that shit off*. We were trapped in a bankrupt city,
rumors of a psychokiller, pandemic, meltdown.
I ate ramen for lunch at my desk and someone down cubicle row said,
"I honestly don't care if the Ethiopians starve to death."

It was enormously popular to quote from *The Art of War* without irony
    or cynicism.
But Nietzsche—all that talk of a growing wasteland—no one wanted to
    hear it.
We were done with malaise, case closed.
It was a bull market and collusion was the watchword.

Waffle House waitresses swore they saw the ghost of Elvis in the small
    hours.
TV preachers damned the diseased then cruised the strips for a boy toy.
It was happy hour over margaritas when Kirk from Payroll said
he was sick and tired of his tax money going to faggot photographers,
and who does this Applethorp asshole think he is anyway?

We were mainlining, every last one of us, even the FBI agents in Arab
   disguise.

Recruiting posters touted travel opportunities: Logging the Amazon,
drilling the Arctic, trip-wiring the isthmus. A gunship ride over Grenada.
Swift boats patrolling the Persian Gulf. Flash fires consuming the
   cedars of Lebanon.
It was sudden death, America's team marching downfield while the band
   played on.

The auto-da-fé was in full burn, edicts pronounced on the hour.
Our lawns were lush and well watered, every gated community insured
by Smith and Wesson, locked and loaded, lined up in the crosshairs.
A landslide kept us on the roller coaster for one more go-round.
Everyone said it was morning in America, right or wrong, love it or leave
   it.

Mister, I wanted to leave it, I truly did. I stopped the car in the middle
   of the tunnel,
got out, and just started walking, a thousand points of light bursting in
   my brain,
all roads leading straight back into the wasteland that wasn't there.

FUGUE

The thought of another road trip
at once entices and appalls.
"Freedom," "escape," "clean
break"—yes, there's that. But also
the endless miles, the tedium
of the American highway—to what end?
Long hours of solitude, soul searching,
melodramatic monologues—sick of yourself.
And yet, in spite of all misgivings,
here you are, loading the trunk,
filling the tank, racing off
into the boundless wasteland.

Ten miles out, magpies watch from wires.
A hundred leagues on, road signs summon towns
but no towns appear. Every exit seems to go nowhere,
a land of remnants: grassy sidetracks petering out,
billboards in tatters, an abandoned mine,
a derelict drive-in theater. You hurtle ahead
into mirage while in the mirror
magpies drop down to scour the trail.

Days on end it's like a movie
of someone else's journey.
Zoom out to an overhead view,
a long shot of the turbulent horizon:
There's your car in the middle distance,
stirring dust, heading straight for calamity:
bad weather   ominous engine noises
fissures   roadblocks   detours

the sudden dead end—no way to back out.

SO WHAT

Crossing the Mississippi bridge for Memphis
heavy rain, dead of night | Miles on the radio
"So What" | | studious piano solo | | brooding
double bass | | sardonic horns crooning
so what | | so what | | so what

Caution: rough road no margin no exit | | so what
Wherever you go, black clouds follow | | so what
An idiot wind taking the world by storm | | so what
The earth goes round, the stars fall down | | so what
Traveling in darkness the only way out | | so what
There's hell to pay in the small hours | | so what
Stare into the abyss, the abyss stares back | | so what
Graceland detour five miles Graceland detour | | so what
Within you, too, the cosmic dark matter | | so what
It is said, All shall be well, and all shall be well | | so what
There's nothing—nothing—more than this | | so what
It is what it is what it is it is | | so what

And now the deserted streets of Memphis | | shuttered diners
forlorn blues bars | | detours around road work
and rain | | rain | | city and delta saturated
with the Dorian mode | | dark in the darkling rain

so what | | so what | | so what

SOUTHBOUND

1.
Newly furloughed from the army,
his backseat rattling with beer cans,
my first ride hauled me
over the rain-pebbled Ohio with a shout:
Back in the South! Thank you, Jesus!

On the Kentucky side he dropped me
where three rugged crosses, rising
from weeds, proselytized wayward souls.

Uncertain where to go next,
thinking only to escape the cold,
I crossed a pasture for the southbound freeway
while a light rain fell, gentle harbinger
of storms to come.

2.
In Tennessee, run-off from
a strip-mined mountain
pooled in the holding plaza
of a truck stop. I stood by,
hoping for a ride, contemplating
puddles where oily rainbows spiraled
in fractal patterns, reflecting the designs
of long-gone mound builders
whose serpentine temples
had mutated here into
a freeway on-ramp.

Up the ramp, a sign
sternly prohibited hitchhiking
beyond the serpent's head.

3.
Huntsville, Birmingham,
Montgomery, Dothan.
Rain fell on Alabama,
a cold white mist filling
the piney woods.

Outside Troy, a chemical smell
pierced the lungs and the Law told me
to move on down the road, vagrancy
not the least bit tolerated in Pike County.
Chased off, too, were the mallards now gliding
silently through the shiver-drizzle
in flight from the distant pop of shotguns.

Feet wet from roadside weeds and the splash
of passing tires I walked and walked
then slept in the shelter
of an evangelical billboard:
GO TO CHURCH or the DEVIL will get you.
All night, a cartoon demon dancing on cloven hooves
threatened me with pitchfork and flames.

4.
Blessèd be the voice in the dash
that did the talking while the driver chewed
his spearmint cud. Crossing Florida's panhandle
we listened to the gospel truth,
the grim driver working his jaws,
nodding his enthusiasm
for this monotone reading of God's word
as mile after mile Jesus called down
storms of woe upon the heads of Pharisees
and spun His inscrutable parables.

Now the sodden skies opened
and poured forth a Biblical rain,
water overflowing marginal ditches

and coursing across the roadbed.
The commandment EAT flared through fog
and my driver swerved down the off-ramp
into a lot of broken shell, leaving me
at the Last Chance Diner with a dollar
and a rebuke: "You best get right
with God, son, you hear?"

5.
My next ride merged with the heavy traffic
bound for Orlando's theme parks.
The radio sang: *still the rain kept falling,
falling all my years*. Alongside the freeway,
wet cattle grazed beneath billboards touting
the simulacra in store at future exits:
charming princes, mermaids, beauties,
beasts, surf shops, thrill rides, gun shows,
the promise of magic kingdoms yet to come.

South of Kissimmee, the white noise
of conspicuous consumption gave way
to a silent landscape I passed through on foot:
clusters of cabbage palms, sawgrass and sinkholes,
cattail-ringed pools, herons still as stalks,
a prairie of water pressed flat
beneath the black sky, storm clouds
moving in from the gulf,
a school of coelenterates trailing
tentacles of rain over the Everglades.
I wandered along the edge
of a land shunned by man,
no sign of shelter, no end in sight
until a battered truck rattled
from an overgrown sidetrack
and the driver waved me over.

Crouched in the bed of the old cracker's pickup,
huddled under plastic with two hounds,

rain stinging my exposed hands, I pondered
the taillights of northbound cars: red as
the eyes of alligators lurking in the mire.
The cracker tapped the cab's rear glass
and with bony finger pointed
off road toward the misting bogs.
At first I saw nothing, then made out
the looming trunks of three burnt-out trees—
charred, twisted, agonized—
making a Golgotha of the swamp.

6.
On the outskirts of Jupiter
the first signs of breakup:
thunderheads fragmenting
into milder mare's tails,
the clouds finally
burning off altogether
at freeway's end,
Miami glistening
like a tide-washed shell.
A city pungent with Cuban coffee
and overripe fruit,
fecund trees and humid decay;
crustacean-pink bungalows
and turquoise motels blinking
in the overwhelming light,
the city simmering, shimmering
in rising waves of heat.

7.
Beyond Miami
the mainland bottomed out
        and broke apart,
            fracturing into coral cays,
    land and sea disputing
the liminal zone.
Trees wandered into saltwater,

crabs clambered over eroding marl,
and I waited among mangroves
alongside Route 1   the Overseas Highway
a rippling and incandescent road
headed out to sea.

CARNIVAL FRUITS AND VEGETABLES
took me island hopping,
gregarious Jamaican driver
generously sharing his gift for gab.
He named the keys as we passed—
Largo   Indian   Duck   Conch.
He waved to each fisherman
keeping watch over the pillars of bridges
that leapt   the gaps   between bay   and sea.
In priestly voice he sang the praises
of shorebirds, foremost the pelican,
symbol, he said, of Christ Our Lord.

Fat Deer Key   Big Pine
     Torch   Ramrod
          Sugarloaf   Shark

the end of the road
bringing me at last to Key West,
with its souvenir shops and tiki bars,
a deranged purgatory for vagabonds,
alms-seekers, grifters, con artists,
sham sea captains too tight to navigate the tides,
cultists singing hosanna to a new age;

and I among them, a wanderer stalled out
at mile zero, the southernmost place,
nowhere else to go and still no answer
to the unsettled question
hanging heavy in the furnace air:
How far is far enough?

ACKNOWLEDGMENTS

Abandoned Mine	"Land of Opportunity"
Barely South	"The Cat Hoarder"
Boulevard	"Shreveport, Louisiana"; "Carrizozo, New Mexico"; "Beatty, Nevada"
Breakwater Review	"Three Thousand Miles: A Haibun Sequence"
Broad River Review	"Uncle Jerry, Missing in Action"
California Quarterly	"Ghost Towns Out West"
Cardinal Sins	"Elk Herd"
Chariton Review	"Variations on a Theme from *North by Northwest*"; "Variations on Five Phrases from Susan Sontag"
Concho River Review	"Off the Rails"; "From Fitzgerald's Notebooks"
Exit 13	"I-10, Westbound"
Little Patuxent Review	"John Berryman, Encyclopedia Salesman"
The Main Street Rag	"Hitchhiking at Night"; "Poem Going Nowhere"
Mudlark	"Southbound"
Naugatuck River Review	"Starlight"
Nimrod	"Hopperesque"
Novus Literary Journal	"Haibun: Meridian, Mississippi"; "Apalachicola, Florida;" "Weatherford, Oklahoma"; "Many Detours"
Peregrine	"Tree of Life"
Rosebud	"Birthplace"
Slipstream	"So What"
Sow's Ear Poetry Review	"Crossing Flagstaff"
Superstition Review	"Uncle Joe, AWOL in Bangkok"
War, Literature, and the Arts	"Uncle Eddie's War Stories"; "Uncle Bill's War,"; "Uncle Jack's War Wound"
Wayne Literary Review	"Down and Out"; "Hitchhiker's Nightmare"; "Urge for Going"

Welter "Reaganomics: A Memoir"
Worcester Review "Double–A Pitching Change"

"Crossing New Mexico" and "Donner Pass Diner" first appeared in the chapbook "American Journey" (Longleaf Press)

ABOUT STEPHEN BENZ

Stephen Benz has published four books of creative nonfiction, including *Topographies* and *Reading the Signs* (both from Etruscan Press). He has also published a book of poems, *Americana Motel* (Main Street Rag Publishing Co.), along with essays in *New England Review*, *Creative Nonfiction*, *River Teeth*, *Boulevard*, and *Best American Travel Writing*. He lives in Albuquerque, where he teaches at University of New Mexico.